Lionel

CN00405165

The Biography of Barcelona's Greatest Soccer (Football) Player

By United Library

https://campsite.bio/unitedlibrary

Introduction

Do you love Lionel Messi?

If you're a fan of soccer (football) and Lionel Messi, then this is the book for you. This biography tells the story of one of the greatest professional soccer players in history. It's packed with interesting facts and anecdotes about Messi's life and career.

Lionel Messi is widely considered to be one of the greatest soccer players of all time. Born and raised in Argentina, Messi began his career with the Barcelona youth team. He made his professional debut with the club in 2004 and has since gone on to score an astonishing 552 goals in 634 appearances. A five-time winner of the FIFA Ballon d'Or, Messi has also been named FIFA World Player of the Year on six occasions.

Messi is currently the captain of both Barcelona and the Argentina national team. As a player, Messi is renowned for his exceptional dribbling ability, vision, and passing. He has frequently been described as a "magician" on the pitch and is widely regarded as one of the best players of his generation. Thanks to his incredible talent and achievements, Lionel Messi has cemented his place as a true legend of the beautiful game.

You'll learn everything there is to know about this amazing athlete – from his early childhood all the way to his record-breaking achievements on the pitch. If you're looking for a comprehensive biography about Lionel Messi, look no further than this book.

Table of Contents

Lionel Messi

Lionel Andrés Messi Cuccittini (Rosario, June 24, 1987), known as **Leo Messi**, is an Argentine footballer who plays as a striker or midfielder. Historical player of Futbol Club Barcelona, to which he was linked twenty years, from 2021 he integrates the squad of Paris Saint-Germain of the French Ligue 1. He is also an international with the Argentina national team, of which he is captain and all-time top scorer.

Often considered the best player in the world and one of the best of all time, he is the only footballer in history to have won, among other distinctions, the Ballon d'Or seven times, six FIFA World Player of the Year awards and six Golden Boots. In 2020, he became the first footballer and the first Argentine to receive a Laureus award, as well as being included in the Ballon d'Or Dream Team.

With Barcelona he has won 35 titles, including ten La Liga titles, four UEFA Champions League titles and seven Copa del Rey titles.

A prolific goal scorer, he holds, among others, the records for most goals in a season, in a calendar year (in 2012, with 86 goals, he entered the Guinness World Records) and in the same club, in addition to being top scorer in La Liga, the Spanish Super Cup, the European Super Cup and the non-European player with the most goals in the UEFA Champions League, as well as top scorer for Barcelona and the Argentine national team. He is the player with the most assists in official matches since records began.

Born and raised in the city of Rosario, at the age of 13 he moved to Spain, where Barcelona agreed to pay for the treatment of the hormonal disease he had been diagnosed with as a child. After a rapid progression through Barcelona's youth academy, he made his official debut for the first team in October 2004, at the age of seventeen. Despite being injury-prone early in his career, by 2006 he had established himself as a key player for the club. His first uninterrupted campaign was the 2008-09 season, in which Barcelona achieved the first treble in Spanish soccer.

In 2009, at the age of twenty-two, he won his first Ballon d'Or and the FIFA World Player of the Year award. Three successful seasons followed, in which he won an unprecedented four consecutive Ballon d'Or awards. So far, his personal best campaign is the 2011-12 season, in which he set the record for most goals in a season, both in La Liga and in other European competitions, and became, in March 2012, his club's all-time top scorer in official competitions.

During the following two seasons, he also suffered injuries and, in 2014, lost the Ballon d'Or to Cristiano Ronaldo, who is considered his rival. He regained his best form during the 2014-15 campaign, in which he surpassed the all-time top scorer records in La Liga and the Champions League and achieved a historic second treble with Barcelona, as well as winning his fifth Ballon d'Or. He would win it again for the sixth and seventh time in 2019 and 2021.

As an Argentine international, Messi has represented his country in ten major tournaments. At the youth level, he won the 2005 U-20 World Cup with the U-20 team, a tournament in which he finished as best player and top scorer, and a gold medal at the 2008 Olympic Games with the U-23 team. Because of his small, left-handed dribbling style of play, he was compared to his compatriot Diego Maradona who, in 2007, declared the teenager his "successor". After making his senior national team debut in

August 2005, at the 2006 World Cup in Germany he became the youngest Argentine to play and score in a World Cup. The following year he played in the Copa America, where he was named best young player of the tournament.

As captain since August 2011, he reached with his team the finals of the 2014 World Cup in Brazil, the 2015 Copa America (competitions in which he was voted best player of the tournament) and the Copa America Centenario, in addition to winning the 2021 Copa America against Brazil at the Maracana and the Finalissima against Italy at Wembley in 2022.

Origins and formation

Lionel Andrés Messi was born on June 24, 1987 at the Hospital Italiano Garibaldi in the city of Rosario, in the province of Santa Fe. He is the third son of Jorge Horacio Messi and Celia María Cuccittini. He has two older brothers, Rodrigo and Matías, and a younger sister, María Sol. His paternal family is originally from the Italian municipality of Recanati, from where his great-grandfather, Angelo Messi, emigrated to Argentina in 1883. His maternal grandmother, Celia Olivera de Cuccittini, encouraged him to dedicate himself to soccer and is the one he thanks after scoring each goal, looking up and pointing to the sky with both hands. Two of his cousins (Maximiliano and Emanuel Biancucchi) are also soccer players. He studied at Elementary School No. 66 "Gral. Las Heras".

When he was just four years old, he started practicing soccer at the Abanderado Grandoli club, located in the south of Rosario, in the Grandoli neighborhood, a few blocks from his home. His first coach was Salvador Aparicio. In 1994, he began training in the lower divisions of Newell's Old Boys. At the age of eight, he was diagnosed with a growth hormone deficiency. For a year and a half, the treatment, which cost 900 dollars a month, was covered by his social security and Acindar, the steel company where his father worked.

In 1995, he played an unofficial tournament with Central Córdoba.

In 1999, the Italian team Como had the opportunity to sign him, but finally did not do so due to difficulties with his family's move. The following year, after being recruited by Federico Vairo in Rosario, Messi went to Buenos Aires to try out for River Plate. Eduardo Abrahamian, in charge of the club's youth divisions, asked for his recruitment, but it never materialized. The reason why he did not join the institution was clarified by the player himself in an interview with *Fox Sports Radio* on May 31, 2019:

On September 3, at the age of thirteen, he gave his first interview to a media outlet in the supplement "Pasión Rojinegra" of the newspaper *La Capital* of Rosario.

Two scouts from Buenos Aires, aware of Messi's move to River, contacted his partner in Barcelona, Horacio Gaggioli, who in turn contacted agent Josep María Minguella. Minguella decided to call Carles Rexach to ask him to try out the player.

On September 17, 2000, coming from Buenos Aires with a stopover in Madrid, Messi arrived with his father at El Prat, Barcelona's airport, where Gaggioli was waiting for them to take them to the hotel, right in front of the Camp Nou. Joaquín Rifé, the youth coach, summoned him to take part in a training session with children in his category, including Cesc Fábregas and Gerard Piqué. In one of these training sessions, which lasted two weeks, he scored six goals and, according to Joan Lacueva, the club's executive in charge of grassroots soccer, "at half time they had to change his team to balance the friendly". However, the club still did not sign him, because they were waiting for Rexach, who had gone to the Sydney Olympics, to return. Finally, a trial was arranged on October 2 at Camp 3, on Rexach's return, and he saw Messi play and resolved the situation: "I arrived with the game started and didn't have time to sit down. It was clear to me that if we didn't sign him, we would regret it," he recalled years later.

Despite the fact that some coaches did not approve of Messi's signing, on December 14 Rexach met at the Club Tennis Pompeia restaurant with Gaggioli and Minguella and drew up an agreement in principle on a paper napkin committing to his signing, which was signed by all parties involved as a contract.

On January 8, 2001, they signed a document in which they secured a job for Messi's father in grassroots soccer (as a way of covering up the teenager's signing) and payment for hormone treatment. The following month, the Messi family settled in Barcelona, first in a hotel and then in an apartment in Les Corts. The mother and siblings returned to Rosario shortly thereafter.

Lower categories

Newell's Old Boys (1994-1999)

Messi played in Newell's youth teams between 1994 and 1999. He was part of the 1987 category, known as "La Máquina '87", coached by Ernesto Vecchio. He made his debut against Pablo VI on April 9, in a match that Newell's won 6-0, with four goals of his own. With the club he won, among other titles, the Friendship Cup of Peru in 1997. In his time at Newell's, he scored 234 goals, with an average of 1.32 goals per game. In a 2014 interview, Vecchio commented: "Watching Leo play at such a young age was really impressive. One could not believe (...) to see a boy with that virtue, that quality, and so small, so tiny, doing so many things with the ball".

F. C. Barcelona (2000-2005)

In 2001, Messi began training with Rodolfo Borrell's Infantil A team, but was later transferred to Infantil B, coached by Xavi Llorens, where he played as a left midfielder or left winger. Being a foreigner, he could not participate in official matches, but he could play in friendlies. He played for the first time in March, away against Amposta, and scored a goal, but in the next game, against Ebre Escola Esportiva on April 21, he fractured his left fibula, so he could not play until June. Shortly after, while descending a staircase, he strained ligaments in his left ankle and missed the rest of the 2000-2001 season. He returned to training with Infantil A in the 2001-2002 season, but was soon promoted to Tito Vilanova's Cadete B, where he scored nine goals in ten games. In the 2002-2003 season he played for Cadete A, coached by Álex García. He played 31 games in which he scored 38 goals and won the League and the Catalonia Cup.

He started the 2003-2004 season on August 8, 2003 in the Juvenil B, in the framework of the Toyota U17 Club World Cup, with Feyenoord from the Netherlands as rival, which the Spaniards defeated 3-1. He played all 90 minutes and gave an assist to Franck Songo'o. On September 14, he made his debut with Juan Carlos Pérez Rojo's Juvenil A, in a 3-0 victory over Hércules. On October 26, in the second matchday of the championship against Gimnastic de Tarragona, he scored four goals in a match for the first time: at 7, 55, 65 and 90 minutes for the 0-7 Barcelona victory. On November 29, he made his debut with Barcelona C against Europa in Spain's Third Division. That year, he played in four categories in four months, in which he went from the youth team to the professional team.

After eleven games with Barcelona C, on March 6, 2004 he played for the first time with Pere Gratacós' Barcelona B against Mataró in the Second Division B. Towards the end of the season, he played six times with Barcelona B and also played games with Barcelona C and the Juvenil A and B teams of the División de Honor Juvenil. On May 15, with Juvenil A, in the second leg of the round of 16 of the Copa del Rey Juvenil against Sevilla, he scored his second *hat-trick*. He scored, in total, 35 goals in 37 official matches with Juvenil B, Juvenil A, Barça C and Barça B, as well as participating in a friendly with the first team.

In the 2004-2005 season, he alternated games in the Second Division B and First Division: he played seventeen games for Barcelona B, scoring six goals, and nine for the first team, scoring once.

Trajectory

Soccer Club Barcelona: First years

Frank Rijkaard, coach of the first team, called Messi and other youth players to play an exhibition match against FC Porto, then coached by José Mourinho, at the inauguration of the Estádio do Dragão in Porto. Thus, on November 16, 2003, at the age of sixteen years and 145 days, and when he had not yet played for Barça B, he played for the first team for the first time. On February 18, 2004, he was called up for another friendly, this time against FC Shakhtar Donetsk.

He began the preseason playing six friendlies with the first team: against Banyoles, Figueres, Palamós at Camp Nou, Hércules, Kashima Antlers and Olympique de Marseille, where he started for the first time. Against Palamós on July 20, in the 74th minute, he scored his first goal, which made it 0-4 in a match that Barcelona won 0-6.

He played his first official match on October 16 against R. C. D. Español, at the Olímpico Lluís Companys stadium, when he replaced Deco eight minutes before the end of the match. At seventeen years, three months and twenty-two days, he became one of the youngest canteranos to debut in La Liga. On October 27 he played for the first time in the Copa del Rey against Gramenet and on December 7 in the 2004-2005 Champions League against FC Shakhtar Donetsk at the Donbass Arena. Towards the end of that year, the newspaper *El País* described him as "the great promise".

Messi scored his first official goal on May 1, 2005, in a La Liga match against Albacete Balompié, after having another goal disallowed for *offside*. At seventeen years, 10 months and 7 days, he became the youngest player to score a goal for Barcelona in that tournament. Bojan Krkić, in 2007, broke this record by scoring a goal on a pass from Messi, in a match against Villareal CF. After five seasons without winning the title, Barcelona became La Liga champions on May 14 with a 1-1 draw against Levante three matchdays before the end of the tournament.

After he won the Golden Ball and the Golden Shoe at the U-20 World Cup, at the beginning of the 2005-06 season he was considered a serious contender to be the revelation player of the year. In the second half of 2005, the newspaper *El Mundo* spoke of a duel between Messi and the young Brazilian Robinho, signed by Real Madrid that same year, whom it considered the future stars of La Liga. In June, Messi signed his first contract as a first-team player, which tied him to the club until 2010 and had a termination clause of 150 million euros, similar to those of Ronaldinho and Samuel Eto'o, players already established in the squad. Due to the interest he had aroused in other European clubs, such as Scotland's Glasgow Rangers, for his performance at the U-20 World Cup and the Joan Gamper Trophy, on September 16 president Joan Laporta decided to increase his salary and extend his contract until 2014, with the same termination clause.

In the 2005-2006 season, the first title Barcelona won was the Spanish Super Cup against Betis. Although Rijkaard had brought him on as a substitute, Messi could not play because the quota of foreigners was already filled and the same thing happened to him in the first five La Liga matches. On August 24, he started the Joan Gamper Trophy against Juventus at Camp Nou. Although Barcelona lost 2-4 in the penalty shootout after a 2-2 draw, his performance was so good that, for the first time, he received a standing ovation when he was substituted and Fabio Capello, Juventus' DT, asked Rijkaard if he would not give him up, saying in the press conference afterwards that "I had never seen a player with such quality at this age and with such personality in such an important shirt". In *Mundo Deportivo*, Andres Astruells wrote that for Messi, whom he defined as "small, incisive" and with "a devilish change of pace", the Trophy had been "his great night" and Santi Nolla stated that it had "catapulted" him. In *El País'* match report, it was noted that "Last night's Gamper will go down in history for having enthroned a masterful footballer who gave a recital", while other Spanish journalists described it as a turning point in the player's career.

So that he could play despite being a foreigner, Barcelona appealed to the Royal Spanish Football Federation to consider him assimilated, but on September 19, the Delegated Commission of the Professional League rejected that concession. Messi, therefore, could not participate in Spanish competitions, although he could participate in the Champions League. The club, then, decided to accelerate his nationalization, which he obtained on September 26. The following day, he played in the 2005-2006 Champions League against Italian side Udinese at the Camp Nou. The fans in the stadium gave him a standing ovation before the game and after his substitution, as well as appreciating his composure with the ball and passing combinations with Ronaldinho.

On November 2, Messi scored his first goal in the Champions League against Panathinaikos, which Barcelona won 5-0. On November 19, in a La Liga match, he started his first match against Real Madrid, which the Catalan team won 3-0, remembered for the applause of the rival fans at the Santiago Bernabéu stadium for Ronaldinho. He played an outstanding role in the Clasico and also provided the assist for the first goal to Eto'o.

In September, he received the Eurochampion award in Italy, which honors the best young player in the world, and in December, the Italian magazine *Tuttosport* awarded him the Golden Boy prize for the best young player in Europe. Messi, with 225 points out of 300, beat Wayne Rooney (127) and Lukas Podolski (74).

Title and consecration at the elite level

In the 2006-07 season, Messi established himself in the starting lineup and scored seventeen times in thirty-six games.

The press highlighted his performance in the round of 16 of the 2005-2006 Champions League on February 22, 2006 against Mourinho's Chelsea at Stamford Bridge, while Diego Maradona, in an interview with the BBC, pointed him out as the one who would "take his place" in Argentine soccer.In a match that Barcelona won 1-2, Messi kicked five times on goal, all between the posts, and converted a goal in the 72nd minute. In the second leg, played at Camp Nou on March 7, he ruptured his left femoral muscle, which prevented him from playing the next seventeen matches. On May 3, Barcelona won La Liga and became European champions on May 17, after beating Arsenal at the Stade de France.

On August 17 and 20, Messi played his first final with the first team, the Spanish Super Cup, which Barcelona beat Espanyol 1-0 and 3-0. He participated in another final on August 25, the European Super Cup, which Barcelona lost to Sevilla. He did not score goals in either competition.

On November 12, in a league match against Real Zaragoza, he suffered a broken left metatarsal that kept him out of the field for three months. He recovered from his injury in Argentina and returned against Racing Santander on February 11, 2007, where he entered in the second half.

In January 2007, his pay was increased to three million euros per year and his contract was extended until 2014.

On March 10, he scored a hat-trick in El Clasico, which was a 3-3 draw with ten men on his team, and became the youngest player to have scored in that match. Not since Romario in 1994 had any other Barcelona player scored a hat-trick in El Clasico and no one had done so since Ivan Zamorano in 1995. Towards the end of La Liga, Messi began to accumulate more goals than he had at the start of the season (11 of his 14 goals in the league season were scored in the last 13 games).

Messi was labeled the "new Maradona" for scoring goals similar to the Argentine player's two most famous ones. On April 18, 2007, he scored two goals in the semifinals of the Copa del Rey against Getafe FC, one of them very similar to Maradona's so-called Goal of the Century against England in the 1986 World Cup in Mexico. The world press compared it to the Argentine 10 and the Spanish newspaper *Marca* called it "Messidona". He ran almost the same distance (62 meters) and eluded the same number of players (six, including the goalkeeper), to score from a very similar position, after running towards the corner flag. At a press conference after the match, his teammate Deco said: "It was the best goal I have ever seen in my life".

On June 9, in the Barcelona derby, he scored a goal similar to Maradona's "Hand of God" goal against England in the quarterfinals of the '86 World Cup. He looked for the ball and connected with his hand to guide it past the goalkeeper, Carlos Kameni. Despite protests from the Espanyol players and replays showing the obvious handball, the goal was validated.

Messi was included for the first time in the FIFA/FIFPro World XI in the striker category. Players such as Francesco Totti and Franz Beckenbauer had declared that they considered him one of the best players in the world. On December 4, Messi came third in the Ballon d'Or voting.

Barcelona reached the semifinals in the 2007-2008 Copa del Rey and the 2007-2008 Champions League, but failed to win any titles. However, Messi scored ten goals in La Liga and six in the Champions League.

Golden era of the club: the "Pep Team".

2008-09: Historic triple win

After two unsuccessful seasons, Barcelona needed to reform, which led to the departure of Rijkaard and the arrival of Pep Guardiola as coach. After the departure also of Ronaldinho, Messi was given the jersey with the number 10. In June 2008, he signed his fourth contract for a salary of 8.5 million euros, which made him one of the club's highest paid, and his termination clause was increased to 250 million.

Ahead of the new season, one of the main concerns remained his frequent muscle injuries, which had sidelined him for a total of eight months between 2006 and 2008. To address the problem, new nutrition and sleep regimes were implemented and Barcelona agreed that he would choose a personal kinesiologist and physiotherapist, who would be supervised by the club's medical staff. As a result, he remained virtually injury-free for the next four years.

Despite his injuries earlier in the year, in 2008 he reached second place in the FIFA Ballon d'Or and the FIFA World Player of the Year award, on both occasions behind Cristiano Ronaldo.

On April 8, 2009, in the first leg of the 2008-2009 Champions League quarter-final, he scored two goals and two assists to help Barcelona beat Bayern Munich 4-0.

On May 2, with two goals from Messi, Barcelona beat Real Madrid 6-2 as visitors, in what was their biggest win at the Santiago Bernabéu. That was the first game in which Messi scored a goal in that stadium and played as a false nine, after Guardiola decided that he would no longer play as a winger and established him as the team's focal point.

On May 13, he scored his first goal in a first-team final and also assisted on the second as Barcelona defeated Athletic Bilbao 4-1 to win the 2008-2009 Copa del Rey after eleven years. Three days later, Barcelona won La Liga without playing.

On May 27, in the Champions League final against Manchester United at Rome's Stadio Olimpico, Messi headed Barcelona's second goal as they won 2-0 and received their third European Cup, thus achieving the first treble in Spanish soccer and the fifth in history, along with Celtic, Ajax, PSV and Manchester United In an interview with Argentine channel TyC Sports in 2019, the player chose that goal as the most important of his career.

In his first uninterrupted campaign, he scored 38 goals in 62 matches, nine of them in the Champions League, making him the top scorer in that edition. Moreover, his goals, added to those of Eto'o (36) and Thierry Henry (26), gave a total of 100 goals in all competitions. 70 of those 100 were scored in La Liga, breaking the record of 66 goals set by Ferenc Puskas (28), Alfredo Di Stéfano (21) and Luis del Sol (17) for Real Madrid in the 1960-1961 season.

2009-2010: Sixth consecutive six-team title and first Ballon d'Or

Messi scored for the first time in the Spanish Super Cup on August 23 against Athletic Bilbao. He scored two of his team's three goals, which went on to win the trophy. On the 28th, at Monaco's Stade Louis II, he set up Pedro, who scored the goal that won Barcelona the European Super Cup 1-0 against Shakhtar Donetsk. On December 18, he chested home the winner in a 2-1 Club World Cup victory over Estudiantes de La Plata. Thus, the *Pep Team*, led by Messi, made Barcelona the first club to win a six-team title.

At the age of twenty-two, Messi was named UEFA Player of the Year, in addition to winning his first Ballon d'Or and the FIFA World Player of the Year award, on both occasions by the largest margin in the history of each trophy.

In September 2009, when his contract was renewed until 2016, with a salary of eleven million euros and a termination clause of 250 million euros, he became the highest-paid footballer in the world.

On March 14, 2010, in a La Liga match against Valencia, he scored his fourth hat-trick for Barcelona, which allowed his team to win 3-0. For the last of his goals he was a candidate for the Puskas award, but lost to Hamit Altintop.

On April 5, in the second leg of the Champions League quarterfinals, Barcelona beat Arsenal 4-1, with all goals scored by Messi, who, with eight goals, was the top scorer of that tournament. The player was praised by several newspapers around the world for this *poker.* Barcelona was eliminated in the semifinals by Inter Milan. On May 16, after beating Valladolid 4-0 with two goals by Messi, Barcelona became La Liga champions.

Messi scored in twenty games and finished the season with 24 goals (including three hat-tricks), a number not reached by a Barcelona player since Ronaldo in the 1996-1907 season. He received the Pichichi (top scorer in La Liga) and the European Golden Shoe.

2010-2011: fifth League and third Champions League

On October 30, Messi secured Barcelona's first trophy of the 2010-11 campaign, the Spanish Super Cup, by scoring a hat-trick in his team's 4-0 victory over Sevilla in the second leg, following a first leg defeat.

On March 8, 2011, he scored two of Barcelona's goals in a 3-1 victory over Arsenal in the last 16 of the Champions League. For his first goal he was shortlisted for the Puskas award, but lost out to Neymar. He scored a brace again in the first leg of the semi-final, a 2-0 win over Real Madrid on April 27. In the final against Manchester United on May 28 at Wembley Stadium, he was a determining factor in his team's play, not only for his goal, but also for his passing, dribbling and dribbling. Barcelona won 3-1 and won its fourth European Cup. Once again, Messi's performance was highlighted by several newspapers in different countries.

Assuming an organizing role, Messi again played a decisive role in the Clasico on November 29, Mourinho's first in charge of Real Madrid, as Barcelona thrashed their rivals 5-0 in another historic drubbing. He helped his team to sixteen consecutive league wins, a record in Spanish soccer, which concluded with another hat-trick against Atletico Madrid on February 5, 2011.

He finished the season with 53 goals and 24 assists in all competitions, making him Barcelona's all-time top scorer in a season. Moreover, with twelve goals, he was the season's top scorer in the Champions League, which allowed him to equal Ruud van Nistelrooy's record of 2002-2003 and become, after Gerd Müller and Jean-Pierre Papin, the third to hold that title for three consecutive times.

His performances for the club during 2010 earned him, on January 10, 2011, the inaugural FIFA Ballon d'Or, a combination of *France Football*'s Ballon d'Or and the FIFA World Player of the Year award, although he was criticized for receiving that award, due to his failure with Argentina at the 2010 World Cup in South Africa.

2011-2012: a record season

He began the campaign by helping Barcelona win the European Super Cup and the Spanish Super Cup. In the latter, on August 17 in a 5-4 win over Real Madrid, he scored twice, taking his tally to eight goals and surpassing Raúl (7) as the top scorer in that competition.

On August 25, he won the inaugural Best Player in Europe award.

On December 18, he scored two goals in the final of the Club World Cup, in a 4-0 victory over Santos, winning the Golden Ball as the tournament's best player.

On January 9, 2012, with almost 50% of the votes, he again received the Ballon d'Or and became the fourth player in history to win it three times, after Johan Cruyff, Michel Platini and Marco van Basten. By then, he was already widely considered one of the best players in history, alongside the likes of Maradona and Pelé.

On February 18, in a La Liga match against Valencia that Barcelona won 5-1, he scored four goals. He scored that number again (two from penalties) on May 5, in the last but one match against Espanyol, which Barcelona won 4-0 and was the last match under Guardiola. With his second *goal* of the season, he reached 50 goals in this competition, surpassing the record in a European league tournament, set by Dudu Georgescu with Dinamo Bucharest (47) in the 1976-1977 season.

On March 7, after scoring five of Barcelona's seven goals in their home win over Bayer Leverkusen in the second leg of the 2011-12 Champions League round of 16, Messi became the first player to score that many goals in a single match in the history of the competition.

On March 20, against Granada at Camp Nou, after scoring a hat-trick to reach 234 goals, he displaced César (232) as Barcelona's all-time top scorer.

On April 3, in the second leg of the quarterfinals, Barcelona beat Milan 3-1 with two Messi penalties and advanced to the fifth consecutive semifinal in its history. The player, meanwhile, scored his 14th goal in that edition and his 50th in that tournament, equaling Raúl, Ruud van Nistelrooy and Thierry Henry in total number of goals and reaching José Altafini's record in the 1962-1963 season, which would be surpassed by Cristiano Ronaldo (17) in 2013-2014. He was also the top scorer for the fourth consecutive time, equaling Gerd Müller's record from the 1976-1077 season.

As he became a combination of a No. 8 (a creator), a 9 (scorer) and a 10 (assist), Messi increased his goal-scoring ability in all club competitions during the 2011-12 season, in which he scored a hat-trick or more on ten occasions. With 50 goals in 31 games, he was also top scorer in La Liga and player with the best goal average (1.61) in a season, two records, while his 68 goals in all competitions surpassed Gerd Müller's 67 in the 1972-73 Bundesliga season, making him the top club scorer in a season. In addition to his goals in La Liga, he scored 14 in the Champions League, 3 in the Copa del Rey, 2 in the Club World Cup, 3 in the Spanish Super Cup and 1 in the European Super Cup, making him, with 73 goals, the all-time top scorer in a season in official competitions. If his nine goals with the Argentine national team are added, the total rises to 82.

Messidependence

2012-2013: with Tito Vilanova

Under the guidance of new coach Tito Vilanova, during the second half of 2012 Barcelona had its best start to a La Liga season with 55 points accumulated at the halfway point of the competition, a record in Spanish soccer. Messi, for his part, scored goals in nineteen consecutive games, something unprecedented in Spanish soccer, and, by scoring a brace on December 9 against Real Betis, he reached 86 goals (74 for his club and 12 with the national team) and thus broke two historical records: César Rodríguez's 190 goals in La Liga, making him Barcelona's all-time top scorer in that competition (192 in 228 games), and Gerd Müller's record for most goals in a calendar year, surpassing his 85 goals scored in 1972 for Bayern Munich (72) and West Germany (13). The German player, in an interview with Sport1 channel, congratulated him for breaking his 40-year record, for which Messi sent him a Barcelona jersey with the number 10, which read "To Gerd Müller/My respect and admiration/A hug". With those 86 goals, he entered the Guinness World Records for the number of goals (club and national team) scored in a calendar year. FIFA, however, alleged verifiability problems and did not recognize the achievement. Messi extended that result in the last matches of La Liga and Copa del Rey (two against Cordoba Club de Fútbol, 2 against Real Madrid and 1 against Valladolid), so that he ended the year with 91 goals. As a favorite, he once again received the Golden Ball, making him the only player in history to win this award four times in a row. On the other hand, he was part of the FIFA/FIFPro World XI for the sixth consecutive year.

In December, he renewed his contract until 2018, with a net salary of €13 million.

On March 17, 2013, he wore the captain's armband for the first time, in a La Liga match against Rayo Vallecano; by then, he had become the tactical focal point of the team to a degree matched only by former Barcelona players Josep Samitier, László Kubala and Johan Cruyff.

Since his evolution to a false nine three years earlier, his participation in the team's attack had increased: from 36.1% of goals (2009-10) to 40.5% (2012-13). This dependence of Barcelona on the Argentine player was pointed out by both Evarist Murtra, a former club manager, and his teammate Andrés Iniesta. In the same vein, Piqué commented that "his presence on the field is enough to boost our morale and our level of play".

2013-2014: with Tata Martino

Messi had an inconsistent start to the season under new coach Gerardo Martino.

On November 10, in a match against Betis at the Villamarín stadium, he suffered his third injury of the season when he hurt his left femoral biceps, which sidelined him for two months. Despite his injuries, he finished second in the Ballon d'Or voting, ending his four-year lead over Cristiano Ronaldo.

On March 13, 2014, Barcelona beat Real Madrid 4-3 with a hat-trick from Messi, who thus added 21 goals and surpassed Di Stéfano (18) as the all-time leading scorer in El Clásico.

For the first time in five years, Barcelona ended the season without a major trophy: on April 9, it was eliminated in the quarterfinals of the Champions League after losing 1-0 to Atletico Madrid, was defeated 2-1 on April 16 in the final of the Copa del Rey by Real Madrid and, on May 17, lost La Liga with a 1-1 draw in the last game against Atletico

Madrid. In the first two games, Messi played well below his level.

After prolonged speculation about his future with the club, Messi in May renewed his contract until 2018, which increased his pay to €20 million gross per year, the highest salary in soccer.

MSN

2014-2015: second treble

Under new coach and former captain Luis Enrique, Messi experienced much of the season injury-free, allowing him to break three more records.

On February 15, in a La Liga match against Rayo Vallecano, he scored two goals in Barcelona's 6-0 victory. He thus reached 337 goals for his club, surpassing Telmo Zarra (335 with Athletic Club) as the top scorer for a Spanish club in the various tournaments.

With a hat-trick against Sevilla on November 22, he became the all-time top scorer in La Liga as, with 253 goals, he surpassed Zarra's record of 251 after fifty-nine years. On November 24, in a Champions League match against APOEL in Cyprus, he reached 74 goals with a hat-trick, making him the all-time top scorer in that tournament and the European Cup. He achieved this record in 91 games, while the previous holder, Raúl, had needed 142 to score 71 goals. A third hat-trick against Espanyol on December 7 made him the top scorer in the Barcelona derby, which his team won 5-1, as he surpassed César's 12 goals.

At the beginning of 2015, Barcelona were perceived to be heading for another disappointing end to the season and there was speculation in the media that Messi would leave the club. The player, for his part, was coming off a year in which he had been at the center of criticism because his performance had not been the best. However, on January 11, in a 3-1 victory over Atletico Madrid, each member of the attacking trident of Messi, Luis Suarez and Neymar, nicknamed "MSN", scored a goal, marking the beginning of a highly successful period.

After five years playing as a false nine, Messi returned to his old position on the right flank at the end of the previous year. From there, he regained his best form, arguably the best of his career, while Suarez and Neymar ended the team's offensive dependence on their star player. With 58 goals and 31 assists from Messi, the trio scored a total of 122 goals in all competitions that season, a record in Spanish soccer.

On May 17, Messi scored in a 1-0 away win over Atletico Madrid, securing his club the La Liga title. In the Copa del Rey final on May 30, Barcelona defeated Athletic Bilbao 3-1 for its sixth double in history. Messi started his goal when he took possession of the ball near midfield and dribbled past four defenders with a spike, before feinting past the goalkeeper to score in a tight space by the near post. The goal was voted the best of his career in a poll conducted by the newspaper *Sport*, while *La Vanguardia* described it as an "impossible goal" that "will go down in the annals of the history of the competition".For that goal, Messi was nominated for the Puskas award, but came in second place.

In the Champions League, Messi was instrumental in his team's play in the round of 16, quarterfinals and semifinals. On May 6, in the first leg of the home semi-final, he scored two of Barcelona's three goals in a 3-0 win over Bayern Munich. His second goal, a lob from Jerôme Boateng, was voted the best of the competition in a vote organized by UEFA. In the final on June 6 in Berlin, beating Juventus 3-1, Barcelona won their second treble and became the first team in history to do so. In his fourth Champions League win, Messi was top scorer (6) and, along with Neymar and Cristiano Ronaldo, top scorer (10) of the tournament, and received for the second time the award for Best Player in Europe by a large majority of votes (49, against three for Luis Suárez and two for Cristiano Ronaldo),

2015-2016: domestic success

On August 11, 2015, Barcelona won its fifth UEFA Super Cup, beating Sevilla 4-5 in extra time. Messi, by scoring a brace, reached three goals in that tournament and became top scorer, along with Oleh Blokhin, Radamel Falcao, Arie Haan, Terry McDermott, Gerd Müller, Rob Rensenbrink, David Fairclough and François Van der Elst.

On September 26, in a match against Las Palmas, Messi tore his left tibial collateral ligament, which prevented him from playing for almost two months.

On January 11, 2016, he won his record fifth Ballon d'Or. At the press conference prior to the award ceremony, he had said, "I prefer a World Cup to five Ballon d'Ors. Collective trophies are above individual ones. It would be the most important thing to win a World Cup" and "I am proud of everything I have achieved at Barcelona. It's always much more difficult to win again once you've achieved everything. It's the ultimate. To be here for the ninth time is great and I'm satisfied with that."

On February 23, against Arsenal in the round of 16 of the 2015-2016 Champions League, he scored, in the last twenty minutes of play, a goal and a penalty with which his team won 2-0. It was the first time that Barcelona was able to win at the Emirates Stadium and that Messi converted against Petr Cech, after having crossed him in six matches. On this, the goalkeeper had said: "It's fantastic, not many can say that they have played so many times against Messi and he has not found a way to score against him".

On May 22, Messi scored both goals in Barcelona's 2-0 overtime victory over Sevilla in the 2016 Copa del Rey final at the Vicente Calderón stadium as the club clinched the domestic double for the second consecutive season. In total, Messi scored 41 goals and provided 23 assists, while Barcelona's attacking trio scored a Spanish record 131 goals in the entire season, which beat their own mark from the previous season.

2016-2017: fourth Golden Boot

On August 14, in the first leg of the 2016 Spanish Super Cup, he played a part in Munir's goal in a 2-0 win over Sevilla at the Sánchez-Pizjuán stadium and, in the second leg on the 17th, he provided an assist for Arda Turan and converted a goal in a 3-0 win. It was his seventh Super Cup win and the first in which he lifted the trophy as captain in the absence of Iniesta, who was injured.

On September 13, in a group stage match of the 2016-2017 Champions League, he scored a hat-trick against Celtic, which lost 7-0 in what was Barcelona's biggest drubbing in the history of that tournament. In the following match with that club, he converted a goal and a penalty (his 100th goal in international championships with the club), with which his team won 2-0 and advanced to the round of 16. Ramon Besa, in *El País*, described him as a "total player" whose "prominence is so absolute lately that he questions not only the opponent's soccer but also Barcelona's own".

On September 21, in a La Liga match against Atlético de Madrid, he tore his right thigh and was sidelined for three weeks.

On February 14, 2017, Barcelona lost 0-4 at the Parc des Princes in the round of 16 against Paris Saint-Germain. However, on March 8, in the second leg at Camp Nou, they won 6-1, an unprecedented feat in the history of Europe's top competition, thus advancing to the quarterfinals and becoming the only Spanish team that could still achieve the treble.

After being eliminated in the quarterfinals of the Champions League by Juventus and being runner-up in La Liga, on May 27 Barcelona won the 2016-2017 Copa del Rey, beating Deportivo Alavés 3-1 in the final, with a goal and assist from Messi. It was Luis Enrique's farewell match as coach and the last official match played at the Vicente Calderón stadium. In total, Messi finished the 2016-17 season with 54 goals and 19 assists, while his 37 goals in La Liga led him to win his third Pichichi and fourth Golden Boot.

Local dominance under Ernesto Valverde and difficult years in the Champions League

2017-2018: domestic double and fifth Golden Boot

On September 19, in a La Liga match against Eibar that Barcelona won 6-1, he scored his fourth *poker* in that competition and surpassed his own 2011-2012 season mark for most goals scored (9) in the first five games.

After Neymar's departure for PSG in August, the MSN, which had scored 364 goals and 211 assists in three seasons, was disbanded.

On October 18, against Olympiacos in the Champions League, Messi reached his 100th goal in all UEFA club competitions. He was the first non-European player to do so and second behind Cristiano Ronaldo, although he did so in 21 fewer games.

On November 25, he renewed his contract with Barcelona until 2021, which stipulated a gross salary of €55 million, with a termination clause of €700 million.

On December 23, he scored a goal in a Clasico played in La Liga that Barcelona won 3-0.

On March 14, 2018, in the quarter-final match against Chelsea that Barcelona won 3-0, he reached with a brace the hundred goals in Champions League. Again, he ranked behind Cristiano Ronaldo, but he did it in 123 games, while the Portuguese needed 144.

On April 21, he scored the team's second goal, his 40th of the season, in the 5-0 win over Sevilla in the 2018 Copa del Rey final and then assisted on Suárez's second goal. This was Barcelona's fourth consecutive title and 30th overall. On April 29, in a La Liga match, Messi, with a hat-trick in a 4-2 away win over Deportivo La Coruña, reached his 30th goal of the season, making him the first player in La Liga history to score at least 30 goals in seven different editions. With this result, and with four games left in the tournament, Barcelona won its 25th league title. On May 6, Messi scored what would be his last goal in the Clasico, as he did not score in the next seven games they played. On May 9, Barcelona, with a goal by Messi, defeated Villarreal 5-1 and thus reached 43 consecutive matches without losing, a record in the history of La Liga.

At the end of the season, with 34 goals, Messi received the Pichichi award and also won his fifth Golden Shoe.

2018-2019: captaincy, tenth League and sixth Golden Boot

On March 14, 2018, against Chelsea in the round of 16 of the Champions League, Messi scored a brace and reached 100 goals in that tournament.

After Iniesta's departure in May, he was named captain of the team for the following season and on August 12, he lifted his first title as captain, the Spanish Super Cup, after a 2-1 victory over Sevilla.

On September 2, for a 2018-2019 La Liga match against Huesca that Barcelona won 8-2, he scored a brace and provided three assists.

On September 18, in the group stage of the 2018-2019 Champions League, in Barcelona's 4-0 win over PSV, he scored a hat-trick, his 42nd with his club and his eighth in Champions League, which allowed him to set a new record in that tournament. On November 28, Barcelona beat PSV

2-1 with a goal by Piqué and another by Messi, who became the player with the most goals with the same team (106) in that competition.

On October 20, in the ninth round of La Liga, he scored and assisted in the 4-2 home win over Sevilla, but had to retire in the 26th minute after hurting his right arm in a fall. Subsequent examinations confirmed that he had fractured his radial bone, which meant he would not be able to play for approximately three weeks.

On March 17, 2019, he scored a hat-trick in the 4-1 win over Betis. For one of those goals, he was a candidate for the Puskás award, but lost to Daniel Zsóri.

On April 16, in the quarterfinals of the Champions League against Manchester United, he scored a brace for his team's 3-0 win, after six years without scoring at that stage of the tournament.

On April 27, against Levante, he came on in the second half and scored the only goal in a 1-0 home win that allowed Barcelona to win its 26th La Liga title three games before the end of the tournament, the first with Messi as captain. He also became, with 416 goals in 449 games, the tournament's all-time top scorer and the player with the most La Liga titles (10) in Barcelona's history and the second in Spanish soccer: he equaled Pirri's number and was second only to Paco Gento (12).

On May 1, he scored a brace in a 3-0 home win over Liverpool in the first leg of the Champions League semifinals. His second goal, from a free kick, his 600th for Barcelona, was chosen by UEFA as the best of the season. Six days later, in the second leg at London's Anfield Stadium, Barcelona were eliminated after losing 4-0. Despite his team's elimination, Messi, with 12 goals, was named Forward of the Season.

On May 19, in Barcelona's final league game of the season, he scored twice in a 2-2 draw away to Eibar (his 49th and 50th goals of the season in all competitions). Thus, with 36 goals in 34 appearances, he received his sixth Pichichi. He also won his record sixth Golden Shoe, his third in a row. He scored his last goal of the season in the 2-1 loss to Valencia in the 2019 Copa del Rey final.

2019-2020: sixth Ballon d'Or and Laureus Award

On April 30, he was awarded the Cross of Sant Jordi, granted by the Generalitat de Catalunya, in recognition of "his fabulous sporting career, which has led him to be recognized as the best footballer of all time". He is the third sportsman to achieve this distinction, after Gemma Mengual and Johan Cruyff.

On August 5, 2019, it was announced that Messi would not participate in Barcelona's tour of the United States, as he had injured his right calf. Later that month, he also did not play the first game of the season, due to the fact that he had not yet recovered.

On September 23, he won The Best 2019 award, on November 25, UEFA included him in the best team of the 21st century and on December 2, he received his unprecedented sixth Ballon d'Or.

In a 2019-2020 La Liga match on December 7 against Mallorca, he scored his 35th hat-trick, surpassing Cristiano Ronaldo as the player with the most hat-tricks in the Spanish top flight. Until that date, Messi had a much greater impact on the game than he has had in recent years at Barcelona, having generated up to 64% of the team's goals.

On December 7, in the sixteenth round of La Liga, he scored his 1100th goal in Barcelona's victory at Camp Nou against Mallorca, with a final score of 5-2. It was in the 82nd minute of the match when, after a pass from Luis Suárez, he scored his third and the team's fifth goal against Malaga goalkeeper Manolo Reina. At home in the 4-1 win over Alavés on 21, he scored his 50th goal (45 for club and 5 for national team) of the calendar year for the ninth time and sixth in a row.

On January 9, 2020, in the semifinals of the Spanish Super Cup, he became the player with the most games played in that competition, as well as reaching his 14th goal.

With Quique Setién as the new coach, Messi moved his position on the pitch to play more as a 10 rather than a false 9, which meant a decrease in his goal scoring and an increase in assists. He scored the winning goal in a 1-0 victory over Granada on January 19, Setién's debut day, but did not score again until February 22, when he converted the sixth and quickest *poker* of his career in a match against Eibar.

On February 17, he became the first soccer player and the first Argentine to receive the Laureus Award for the best sportsman of the year, after six previous nominations.

In the 2-2 draw against Real Madrid on June 30, he scored his 700th goal from the penalty spot (630 for his club and 70 for the national team), a feat only achieved by Romario, Josef Bican, Ferenk Puskás, Pelé, Gerd Müller and Cristiano Ronaldo. On July 19, in the last game of the season, after his brace in the 5-0 win over Alavés, he was top scorer (25) and best provider of assists (21) in La Liga, beating Xavi's record of 20. By winning his seventh Pichichi trophy for the fourth consecutive time, he surpassed Zarra in the number of awards and equaled Di Stéfano and Hugo Sánchez, who also received it in four consecutive editions. However, Barcelona lost the league title to Real Madrid.

On August 8 at the Camp Nou, in the second leg of the round of 16 of the 2019-2020 Champions League against Napoli, he scored two goals (the second disallowed by VAR) and won a penalty that Luis Suarez took. His goal was voted by UEFA the best of the season. With a 3-1 victory, Barcelona qualified for the quarterfinals against Bayern Munich. On August 15, Messi suffered the worst defeat of his entire career when Bayern Munich crushed Barcelona 8-2 in a single match in Lisbon.

August 2020: desire to leave Barcelona

Following Messi's growing dissatisfaction with Barcelona's management on and off the field, the club announced that the player had sent him "a document expressing his desire to leave" on August 25, 2020. The news garnered significant media coverage and even generated comments from current and former teammates (who supported Messi's statement) and the Catalan president, Quim Torra. On August 26, Barcelona sporting director Ramon Planes reiterated the club's desire to "build a team around the most important player in the world" and stated that Messi could only leave if a buyer paid his €700 million termination clause. An early termination option available in the contract (which would have allowed him to leave the club for free) could only be exercised if Messi had communicated his decision to Barcelona by May 31, 2020, although the player's representatives argued that the deadline should be set for August 31, due to the postponement of the 2019-2020 season. On August 30, La Liga issued a statement indicating that the contract and termination clause were still active.

On September 4, Jorge Messi issued a statement in response to La Liga stating that the termination clause "is not valid when the termination of the contract is by unilateral decision of the player from the end of the 2019-20 season," as stated in Messi's contract with Barcelona;

moments later, La Liga reiterated its statement published on August 30.That night, in an interview with Goal, Messi announced that he would continue at Barcelona for the final year of his contract and that he had informed the club of his desire to leave several times and that the president, Josep Bartomeu, had said he could decide at the end of each season whether to stay or leave, but Bartomeu was referring only to the termination clause. This left the player with two options: stay or go to court against the club, but he stated, "I would never go to court against the club of my life."

Time with Ronald Koeman and farewell to the club

2020-2021: all-time top scorer at club level

In September 2020, Messi joined the preseason training under the orders of the new coach, Ronald Koeman. That same week, he took part in a friendly against Nástic de Tarragona.

On September 19, two days after the twentieth anniversary of his arrival at Barcelona, won the Joan Gamper Trophy with the team, the eleventh in his personal trophy cabinet. On the 26th of the same month, he played against Villarreal in the first La Liga match of the season, thus becoming, together with Xavi and Carles Rexach, the player with the most seasons at the club (17).

On November 7, in the ninth round of La Liga, Barcelona beat Betis 5-2 at Camp Nou. By scoring his second goal, Messi became the top scorer in the history of first division soccer in a single league, and caught up with Bican, who had 447 goals (417 with Slavia Prague and 30 with MFK Vitkovice) in the Czechoslovakian league. On December 14, he was included as a right winger in the historic Ballon d'Or *Dream Team.* On the same day, it was the 20th anniversary of his first contract with the club.

On December 17, FIFA included him in the FIFA/FIFPro World XI ideal team of the year. Two days later, in the fourteenth round of La Liga, Barcelona faced Valencia at home with a final score of 2-2. Messi, after missing a penalty against Jaume Domenech, headed in the same play and scored the first goal in the 49th minute of the first half. He thus equaled the 643 goals scored by Pelé with Santos. The Brazilian player congratulated him on

Instagram for the achievement and for his career at the club, while expressing his admiration.

On December 21, he received his seventh Pichichi trophy, the fourth in a row, which brought him level with Hugo Sánchez, winner of the award between 1984 and 1989, and Gerd Müller and Eusebio as the most top scorer in their respective leagues.

He surpassed Pele's record as the top scorer in the history of soccer for a single club on December 22, after scoring the last goal in Barcelona's 3-0 away win over Valladolid.

In 2021, he had the second-best league start of his career, with four goals before January 10.

In January, the IFFHS named him Conmebol's best player of 2020, best playmaker of the 2011-2020 decade, as well as including him in the best world and Conmebol teams of the 2011-20 decade. On February 7, he was named best player of the 2011-2020 decade.

On January 17, in the Spanish Super Cup final won 3-2 by Athletic Club, Messi received his first red card at Barcelona after a cross with Asier Villalibre.

On January 31, his 2017 renewal contract with Barcelona was published, which was, until that date, the largest in the history of the sport.

On February 16, 2021, in the round of 16 of the 2020-2021 Champions League at Camp Nou, Messi scored the only goal for the home team, which lost 4-1 against PSG. On March 10, he scored the goal for the 1-1 draw and missed a penalty in the second leg, in which Barcelona was eliminated and which would be his last match in that competition with that club.

On March 21, against Real Sociedad at the Reale Arena, Messi displaced Xavi as the player with the most official matches in the club's history (768 vs. 767) and scored his 700th goal for the club (663 in official matches and 37 in friendlies).

On April 17, in the final of the Copa del Rey, played at the La Cartuja stadium in Seville, Barcelona beat Athletic 4-0 with two goals from Messi, who won his first cup as captain. He was also named player of the match, equaled, along with Piqué and Sergio Busquets, the seven trophies won by Piru Gaínza and José María Belauste and, with nine goals, surpassed Zarra as top scorer in finals, as well as becoming the competition's all-time leading scorer.

On May 16 at Camp Nou, he played against Celta de Vigo and scored, with a header, his 474th goal in La Liga, which made him the all-time top scorer in that tournament. This would also be his last match with Barcelona, his 778th, and in which he scored his 672nd goal. That number of goals earned him recognition by the IFFHS as the top scorer in the history of a single club in February 2022.

On May 21, Koeman gave him permission to bring forward his vacation, so he did not play in the last La Liga match against Eibar. Barcelona finished third and Atlético de Madrid were champions.

Without having clarified whether or not he would renew his contract, which expired on June 30, on May 26 he traveled to Argentina to join his national team and begin training for the 2022 World Cup qualifiers and the Copa América.

Farewell to Barcelona

Although La Liga had approved Messi's new five-year contract with Barcelona (in which the player agreed to reduce his salary during the first year), at the last minute

Laporta informed Jorge Messi that, due to budget issues, he could not renew the player. On August 5, 2021, Barcelona announced that it could not keep Messi, as doing so would mean exceeding the spending cap allowed by the Spanish league. Messi played a total of 778 official matches, scored 672 goals and won 35 titles (including ten Leagues and four Champions Leagues).

In a conference at the club's facilities, the player stated: "I gave everything for this club, from the first day I arrived until the last, I never imagined having to say goodbye because I didn't think about it. I did everything I could to stay and it was not possible".

Paris Saint-Germain

On August 10, Paris Saint-Germain announced Messi's arrival through a video on its social networks. The player signed a two-year contract with an option to extend it for one season, with a salary of 36.5 million euros and would wear the number 30, the same number with which he debuted at Barcelona.

On the 29th of the same month, he played his first match with the team against Stade de Reims, on the fourth matchday of Ligue 1. He entered the field in the 65th minute, replacing Neymar. The match ended 0-2 in favor of the Parisian team, with two goals from Mbappé. On September 28, he scored his first goal for PSG, in the 74th minute after a one-two with Mbappé, in the second matchday of the Champions League Group A against Guardiola's Manchester City, with the Parisians winning 2-0 at the Parc des Princes.

On October 19, he scored his first brace, the second goal in the 74th minute, after a foul on Mbappé in the opponent's box, a penalty he scored Panenka-style. It was for the third Champions League qualifier against Jesse Marsch's Leipzig, with the home side winning 3-2 in Paris.

On November 20, in the fourteenth matchday, he scored his first goal in Ligue 1. The final score was 3-1, after a 1-0 comeback against Nantes. Up to that date, the team was still leading the competition, with a ten-point lead over Lens. On the 28th of that month, he scored a hat-trick of assists against Saint-Étienne, two to Marquinhos and one to di Maria, in a 1-3 victory for the visitors at the Geoffroy-Guichard.

The following day, he won his seventh Ballon d'Or and his eighth Pichichi.

On December 7, on the last qualifying matchday for the round of 16 of the Champions League, he scored another brace in his team's 4-1 win over Bruges. In that match, he equaled Cristiano Ronaldo as the player who has scored the most goals in European competition (38) and, with 758 professional goals, surpassed Pelé (757).

In December, the IFFHS included him in the Conmebol team of the year and recognized him as the best player and playmaker in that confederation.

On January 2, 2022, Messi tested positive for coronavirus during his vacation in Argentina. After being in isolation since December 28 and testing negative in a new PCR, he was able to return to Paris and resume training, although no new tests were performed to rule out sequelae. On the 22nd of that same month, he was called up against Reims, in what was his first match of the year, this time for the 22nd date of the Ligue 1. He came on as a substitute in the second half of the match, which ended 4-0 for the Parisian team.

On January 17, he was included in the FIFA/FIFPro World XI for the 15th consecutive time.

On February 15, in the Champions League 2021-22 round of 16 series against Real Madrid, he missed a penalty in the first leg, which ended in a 1-1 draw. His performance received harsh and controversial criticism from French media, such as *L'Équipe*, which rated him a 3. In the second leg at the Santiago Bernabeu on March 9, PSG started winning with a goal by Mbappé, but lost due to a hat-trick by Benzema. The following game, at home to Bordeaux, both Messi and Neymar were booed and whistled.

With 125 goals, he was second only to Cristiano Ronaldo, with 140, on the list of all-time UEFA Champions League top scorers. Both players are the only ones to have scored more than 100 times in the history of the competition.

On April 23, he won his first title with PSG by winning the 2021-22 Ligue 1.

National team

Lower categories

In 2002, Jorge Messi sent Hugo Tocalli, in charge of Argentina's youth divisions, a video compilation of his son's plays. Despite recognizing the teenager's qualities, the coach replied that he could not include him in the squad, because he had already defined the team for the following year's World Cup in Finland, but that he would keep him in mind for another competition. In 2003, however, and although he knew that the Spanish Football Federation wanted to sign him for their national team, he did not call him up for the U-20 World Cup in the United Arab Emirates either. On March 30, 2004, he met with AFA president Julio Grondona and, following a suggestion by José Pékerman (who had seen Messi against Alcorcón), proposed to organize a friendly match to prevent any possibility of him playing for Spain. In April, Messi finally received a faxed summons for a training session in June in Ezeiza. The player had already declined, around 2003, repeated offers to play for Spain because he wanted to represent his country.

On June 29, 2004, almost unknown in his country, he made his debut at the Diego Armando Maradona stadium in Buenos Aires, in the U-20 category, in a friendly match against a Paraguayan U-22 team assembled for the occasion and refereed by Gabriel Brazenas. He came on in the second half for Ezequiel Lavezzi and scored a goal and made two assists in a match that ended in an 8-0 victory for Argentina. On July 3, against Uruguay at the Suppicci stadium in Cologne, he scored a *brace in* another friendly that Argentina won 4-1. With only these two games played, on December 27 Tocalli called him up for the South American U-20 Championship early the following year.

South American Under-20 2005

In January 2005, he participated in the South American U-20 Championship in Colombia, his first competition with the Argentine national team. In the first game against Venezuela, he entered in the second half and scored a goal, then a *brace* in the 4-0 win over Bolivia and a goal in the 6-0 win over Peru.

Argentina advanced to the final hexagonal, and on the last date, they played the classic of America against Brazil, which they won 2-1 with a goal by Messi. They finished in third place and qualified for the World Cup tournament to be held in the Netherlands.

2005 U-20 World Cup

In June 2005, with Francisco Ferraro as coach, Messi participated in the U-20 World Cup in the Netherlands. He was not a starter in the match against the United States, where he came on in the second half, but he played in the other six matches. During the first round, he scored a goal in the 2-0 win against Egypt, and gave an assist to Neri Cardozo in the 1-0 win against Germany. In the round of 16 he scored the 1-1 in the 2-1 win against Colombia, in the quarterfinals he scored a goal and an assist in the 3-1 win against Spain, in the semifinals he scored a goal in the 2-1 win against Brazil and in the final against Nigeria he scored a *brace for* his team to win 2-1. At the end of the championship, he received the Golden Shoe and the Golden Ball. Since then, comparisons with Maradona have grown even stronger.

2008 Olympic Games

On May 24, 2008, Messi played for the first time with the U-23 national team, coached by Sergio Batista, in a friendly against Catalonia, which Argentina won 1-0.

On June 17, Barcelona informed the AFA that it would not loan Messi for the Beijing Olympics because it considered that, as it was not an official FIFA competition, the regulations did not oblige it to do so and because it wanted to have "one of the key players of the team" in the Champions League preliminaries. The AFA then requested the intervention of FIFA, which ruled that it was obligatory to release players under 23 years of age. Consequently, on July 3, the coach included him in the squad that would play in Beijing, with the idea that he would be his "main offensive card". As Barcelona did not let up, Jacques Rogge, president of the International Olympic Committee, announced on July 19 that, if they continued their refusal, the club would not be able to count on Messi until August 24, while FIFA president Joseph Blatter demanded four days later that he let the player go. Following FIFA's final ruling in favor of the AFA on July 30, Barcelona decided to take the dispute to the Court of Arbitration for Sport (CAS), which on August 6 overturned the mandatory release of the player. Messi, meanwhile, had traveled to Beijing on July 31, because Batista had said he could no longer wait for him. Finally, on August 8, Txiki Begiristain, Barcelona's technical secretary, announced that he had agreed with Grondona that the player would be allowed to remain in Beijing, if the AFA paid for medical insurance in case of injury and did not call him up for any friendly matches during the season.

On August 7, against Ivory Coast, Messi scored the first goal in the 43rd minute and assisted Lautaro Acosta in the 86th minute. Argentina won 3-1. The second match was against Australia on August 10, with Argentina winning 1-0 with a goal by Lavezzi and an outstanding participation of Messi. On August 13, Messi did not take part in the match against Serbia, as Batista had decided to save him for the quarterfinals.

In the quarterfinals against the Netherlands, Messi scored the first goal, after eluding the goalkeeper. After the opponent's equalizer, in the last minute of the first additional time, he gave a pass to Angel Di Maria, who scored another goal. On August 19, against Brazil, Messi played a very good match, which ended 3-0 with two goals by Sergio Agüero and one by Juan Román Riquelme.

On August 23, after beating Nigeria 1-0 at the National Stadium, with Messi assisting Di Maria's goal, the Argentine players received the Olympic gold medal.

Absolute selection

The Pékerman era

First calls (2005-2006)

On August 2, 2005, Pékerman called up Messi for the first time to play with the senior national team. The player made his debut on August 17 in a friendly against Hungary, where he came on in the 63rd minute for Lisandro López, but only 47 seconds later he was sent off by referee Markus Merk after clashing with defender Vilmos Vanczák.

On September 3, 2005, he played his first official match in the 2006 World Cup qualifiers against Paraguay.

In a friendly against Qatar on November 16, he provided his first assist, allowing Riquelme to open the scoring in a 3-0 win, and on March 1, 2006 he scored his first goal in a friendly against Croatia at the St. Jakob Park stadium in Basel, which Argentina lost 3-2. He also played a very good match on May 30 in a friendly against Angola, won 2-1 by Argentina at the Arechi stadium in Salerno.

World Cup 2006

On May 16, 2006, Pékerman confirmed that he had included Messi in the list of twenty-three to play in the World Cup in Germany that same year. The player, aged eighteen years and 357 days, became the youngest Argentine player to participate in a World Cup. He arrived at the tournament after overcoming a tear he had been carrying since March, so Pékerman had not yet decided whether or not he would be a starter. He made his debut in the World Cup in Argentina's second match, against Serbia and Montenegro. He entered the field in the second half, gave an assist to Hernán Crespo and scored the final 6-0 in the 88th minute, making him the youngest Argentine to score a goal in a World Cup. He started the third group match against the Netherlands (0-0) and, in the round of 16 against Mexico, he came on in the 84th minute and played the entire extra time in which Argentina won 2-1. However, he did not play in the quarter-final against Germany, in which Argentina was eliminated on penalties. A large part of both specialized journalists and general opinion criticized Pékerman's decision, who announced his resignation at the post-match conference. He was succeeded by Alfio Basile, who was appointed in August and took over in September.

Basile Stage

On September 3, 2006, Messi played in Basile's debut match as coach, a friendly against Brazil in London, which Argentina lost 3-0. He also played in the following friendly, on October 11 against Spain at the Nueva Condominas stadium, which Argentina lost 2-1.

America's Cup 2007

On June 5, 2007, in a friendly against Algeria, Messi scored his first brace for the national team.

In the Copa America, Argentina defeated the United States 4-1, where Messi gave an assist to Crespo and was substituted by Tevez after 79 minutes. Against Colombia he caused the 1-1 penalty and participated in Riquelme's second goal. The score ended 4-2 in favor of Argentina. In the third match, this time against Paraguay, Messi entered the field in the 64th minute in place of Esteban Cambiasso. The match ended 1-0 in favor of Argentina with a goal by Javier Mascherano.

In the quarterfinals, Argentina thrashed Peru 4-0, with Messi scoring the second goal of the match. In the semifinals, Messi scored a Vaseline goal against Mexico in

Argentina's 3-0 victory. After the match, Basile said: "Only geniuses are capable of scoring a goal like the one Messi scored. The stadium had to be closed. In the final, Argentina lost to Brazil 3-0, with a counter-attacking goal by Roberto Ayala.

Messi was voted best young player and a member of the "ideal eleven".

On October 16, 2008, after losing 1-0 to Chile in the South American qualifiers the day before, Basile resigned as coach. He was succeeded by Diego Maradona.

Maradona Stage

On March 28, 2009, in his first official match as DT, the 11th date of the qualifying rounds against Venezuela at the Monumental stadium in Buenos Aires, Maradona decided to give Messi the number 10 jersey. Messi was fundamental in the match that Argentina won 4-0: he led the attacking trio he formed with Tévez and Agüero, scored a goal and provided an assist for the second one. The Argentine media highlighted his play, as well as the interest generated by the simultaneous presence of the two "10" in the team.

World Cup 2010

Messi arrived at the World Cup in South Africa under great pressure, as he was considered by many to be Maradona's successor and his campaign with Barcelona was shaping him up to be the great figure of the World Cup.

The first match of the group stage was on June 12 against Nigeria, where Argentina won 1-0 with a goal by Gabriel Heinze. In the second match, against South Korea, which Argentina won 4-1, Messi had a remarkable performance, despite not scoring goals. For the next match against Greece, and in the absence of Mascherano in the squad, Maradona appointed Messi as captain, who, at the age of twenty-two, became the youngest Argentine to play that role in a World Cup. Argentina won 2-0 with goals by Demichelis and Martín Palermo. Messi was named Budweiser Man of the Match. In the round of 16 against Mexico, Argentina won 3-1. In the quarterfinals, Argentina was eliminated after losing 4-0 against Germany.

On July 27, the AFA announced that its steering committee had "unanimously" agreed that Maradona would not continue as coach. He was succeeded by Batista who, after three months as interim coach, was appointed on November 2.

Batista Stage

America's Cup 2011

On July 1, 2011, the first match of the Copa América, held in Argentina, was played between the local team and Bolivia, which ended 1-1. The members of the national team were criticized by the press for the low level of play: *La Nación* published that Messi had not played as a nine and that, "confused", he had not been able to associate with any of his teammates; *Olé, on the* other hand, pointed out that he had not been a leader and that the whole team had been outplayed by a "much inferior" rival. On July 6, after the goalless draw against Colombia at the Brigadier General Estanislao López Stadium in Santa Fe, Messi, who had had a bad game, was heavily criticized by Argentine fans, who demanded that he play as he did at Barcelona.

Criticism eased after Messi provided two assists in the match against Costa Rica on July 11, which Argentina won 3-0 with two goals from Agüero and one from Di María to qualify for the second round.

In the quarterfinals, Uruguay beat Argentina in the 5th minute with a goal by Perez, but Messi assisted Gonzalo Higuain for the equalizer. After extra time, Uruguay won 4-5 on penalties.

Despite not scoring goals, Messi had the most assists (three) and was voted player of the match against Bolivia and Costa Rica. The Argentine team was harshly criticized after the defeat against Uruguay, which was also Batista's last match as coach.

After the AFA fired Batista on July 25, Alejandro Sabella was appointed the new head coach of the Argentine national team on August 5.

Sabella Stage

2014 World Cup Qualifiers

In September 2011, Sabella appointed Messi as captain to replace Mascherano. The player made his debut in his new role on the 2nd of that month in a friendly against Venezuela at the Yuba Bharati Krirangan Stadium in Calcutta, which Argentina won 1-0.

On October 7, in the first match of the 2014 World Cup qualifiers at the Monumental stadium against Chile, Messi scored the second goal in a match that ended 4-1 in favor of his team. It was his first goal in two and a half years, after sixteen official matches without scoring. On October 11 against Venezuela, practically all the players performed poorly and lost 1-0.

On November 11, they played another match against Bolivia. There was great expectation to win the match, as they were playing against a rival that, so far, had never been able to get a point in Buenos Aires. The score was opened by the visiting team after a mistake by Demichelis, which Marcelo Martins took advantage of by anticipating him and stealing the ball in the Argentinean area. Messi had a quite outstanding performance in the first half, where he assisted Higuaín in the first goal, which was incorrectly disallowed. Finally, Lavezzi tied the game, but many of the Argentine fans left the stadium disappointed.

On November 15, in the 2-1 victory over Colombia, the rosarino was the star of the match, scoring the equalizer and being instrumental in the second goal, scored by Agüero. After the match, criticism of Messi diminished, but he was still criticized for not being able to *shine* playing for his country as he did for his team.

On February 29, 2012, he scored his first *hat-trick* with the national team in a friendly against Switzerland. On June 2, in the fifth matchday, the Argentine team beat Ecuador 4-0 with his goal.

On June 8, in a friendly against Brazil's U-23 team in New Jersey, Messi scored his second hat-trick for the national team. His last goal broke the 3-3 draw and Messi left the stadium to a standing ovation. In another friendly against Germany on August 15, he scored a goal in the match that ended 3-1 in favor of Argentina.

On September 7, against Paraguay at the Mario Alberto Kempes Stadium in Córdoba, he scored his first goal from a free kick for the national team, which won 3-1. On the eighth matchday, Argentina's performance in Lima against Peru, where they drew 1-1. On October 12, in the Clasico del Rio de la Plata, Argentina beat Uruguay 3-0 with two goals by Messi, the second from a free kick. On the 16th, Argentina beat Chile 2-1 with a goal by Messi, who reached Gabriel Batistuta's record of twelve goals in a calendar year. Argentina played its last match on November 14, a friendly with Saudi Arabia that ended 0-0.

The qualifying rounds resumed on March 22, 2013. Argentina hosted their Venezuelan counterparts at the Monumental for the eleventh matchday. In the match, which ended 3-0, Messi scored a goal and made two assists. In the next three qualifying rounds, Argentina drew with Bolivia, Colombia and Ecuador in Quito, at high altitude. On June 14, Messi became the second all-time leading scorer of the national team, along with Hernán Crespo, when he scored a hat-trick in a friendly match against Guatemala.

On September 10, 2013, he scored two goals from penalty kicks and provided an assist to Agüero in Argentina's 2-5 win over Paraguay at the Defensores del Chaco stadium in

Asunción. With this result, the Argentine national team qualified for the World Cup with two games left to play, in addition to being in first place in the Conmebol qualifiers.

Due to an injury to his right femoral biceps at the end of September, Messi was unable to play in the last two games in October against Peru and Uruguay. Even so, he finished as the second top scorer in the qualifiers.

World Cup 2014

On June 15, in Argentina's first match at the Brazil 2014 World Cup, against Bosnia-Herzegovina, Messi scored the second goal, after a return on a one-two with Higuaín. On June 21, Argentina faced Iran, where Messi scored his second goal of the tournament in the 91st minute: he scored with a long-range shot outside the big box at the far post, in front of a very populated Iranian defense throughout the match. On June 25, Argentina faced Nigeria in the last match of the group stage. The result was 3-2 in their favor, with Messi's first double in a World Cup: the first goal in the 3rd minute and the second in the 45th minute from a free kick.

On July 1, Argentina played Switzerland in the round of 16. After a 0-0 draw after 90 minutes, in the 118th minute of overtime, Messi assisted Di María in the goal. Argentina managed to advance to the quarterfinals, where on July 5 they faced Belgium. The final score was 1-0 in favor of Argentina, with a goal in the 8th minute, scored by Higuaín.

On July 9, after twenty-four years without reaching the semifinals, Argentina played against the Netherlands. The score was a 0-0 draw after 90 minutes, so it was necessary to go to overtime and then to a penalty shootout, where Messi scored the first goal in a 4-2 result in favor of Argentina.

On July 13, Argentina played the final against Germany at the Maracana stadium. After a 0-0 tie, extra time was played with Mario Götze scoring a goal in the 114th minute. Germany was champion and Argentina was runner-up.

Messi was voted Player of the Match against Bosnia-Herzegovina, Iran, Nigeria and Switzerland. Moreover, with four goals in seven games and one assist, he received the Golden Ball of the World Cup.

On July 29, Sabella resigned as coach. Under his management, Messi, with 25 goals in 32 games, was the team's top scorer, in addition to surpassing his goal averages with other coaches: 0.78 against 0.20 (Pékerman), 0.33 (Basile), 0.36 (Batista) and 0.18 (Maradona).

Martino Stage

On August 14, 2014, Gerardo Martino took over as the new coach of the Argentine national team. He led his first game on September 3, a friendly against Germany in Düsseldorf, in which Messi did not play due to injury. Messi did take part in the following two friendlies: the Superclásico de las Américas on October 11 at the National Stadium in Beijing, where he missed a penalty and Argentina lost 2-0, and on October 14 against Hong Kong at the Hong Kong Stadium where, in just half an hour of play, he provided an assist and scored two of the goals that helped Argentina win 7-0.

America's Cup 2015

On June 13, 2015, in the group stage against Paraguay, Messi scored in the first half and put a momentary 2-0 in favor of his team in a match that ended 2-2. Four days later, he played against Uruguay, which Argentina won 1-0. In both matches he was elected MVP of the match, although he only accepted it on the second occasion. In the last match of the round, which ended 1-0 against Jamaica, he reached 100 caps for his national team. He thus became one of the youngest Argentine players to reach that mark, along with Javier Zanetti, Roberto Ayala, Javier Mascherano and Diego Simeone.

On June 27, in the quarterfinals against Pékerman's Colombia, he scored the first of the penalties that Argentina used to win 5-4 after a 0-0 draw. On June 30, in the semifinals against Paraguay, he made three assists in a match that Argentina won 6-1. In the final against Chile, the Argentine team tied 0-0 after 120 minutes, but lost 4-1 on penalties. Messi was named Player of the Tournament, but refused to receive the award.

America Centenario Cup

Under Martino's leadership, on June 6, 2016, Argentina played against Chile in its first match at the Copa America Centenario, but Messi did not play because he had been injured in a friendly against Honduras. Argentina won 2-1, with goals from Di María and Ever Banega. On June 10, against Panama, Messi came on in the 61st minute to replace Augusto Fernández and scored a *hat-trick in a* match Argentina won 5-0, with two more goals from Nicolás Otamendi and Agüero. On June 18, in the quarter-final match against Venezuela, he reached 54 goals and equaled Batistuta as Argentina's all-time top scorer. He surpassed that mark three days later, in the semifinal against the United States, where he provided two assists and scored a goal from a free kick, in a match that Argentina won 4-0.

On June 26, Argentina faced Chile again in the final. After a goalless draw in 120 minutes, the Chilean team won on penalties. Despite his very good performance throughout the competition and having played a good game, Messi missed his penalty kick, the first of the series.

Martino resigned as coach on July 5.

Resignation and return

In an interview moments after the Copa America Centenario final, Messi announced his retirement from the Argentine national team, a decision he had not even told his teammates in the locker room. He claimed that he "already tried too hard" (in reference to his attempts to win a tournament with his national team):

However, on August 12 of the same year, he confirmed in a press release his return to the national team and that he would also participate in the World Cup qualifiers.

2018 World Cup Qualifiers

Breaking with the tradition that had prevailed for years in the Argentine national team, the defeat in the Copa América 2015 did not mean the departure of Martino, despite what most fans and journalists announced, and continuity and his long-term project were maintained. Messi's first commitment after the Copa América was a tour of the United States in preparation for the 2018 World Cup qualifiers, which included two friendlies against Bolivia and Mexico. On September 4, against Bolivia, Messi came on 19 minutes into the second half and on the second ball he touched, he scored a header to make it 5-0 and, nine minutes later, on the third ball he touched, he scored his second goal, where he dribbled the goalkeeper and made it 6-0, the final result was a 7-0 victory. Thanks to this *brace*, he became the first Argentine player in history to score goals against all South American teams, a record only held by three other South American players. On September 8 against Mexico, Argentina was trailing 0-2, but Agüero scored the equalizer in the 85th minute and Messi scored the equalizer in the 89th minute. On the 26th, he suffered an injury in a match with Barcelona, so he missed the qualifying matches against Ecuador and Paraguay in October, and Brazil and Colombia in November.

On August 5, 2016, Edgardo Bauza was appointed new coach. In his first press conference, he said he would travel to Spain to talk to Messi, although with no intention of convincing him to return.

On September 1, Messi scored the only goal in Argentina's victory over Uruguay. On September 6, due to an adductor injury, he was unable to play against Venezuela. At the end of that month, he tore the adductor in his right thigh, so he did not play in the October matches against Peru and Paraguay. Bauza called him up again on October 25.

On November 10, Argentina lost 3-0 away to Brazil. On November 15, at the Bicentenario stadium, he scored a goal and provided two assists in the 3-0 win against Colombia.

On March 23, 2017, already in the second round of qualifying, he scored the goal with which Argentina won 1-0 against Chile at the Monumental stadium. Five days later, hours before the match against Bolivia in La Paz, FIFA, acting ex officio, issued a statement in which it sanctioned him for four matches, for having insulted the assistant referee of the match against Chile, Emerson Augusto de Carvalho, despite the fact that neither he nor the referee Sandro Ricci had reported it in the minutes.

On April 11, Bauza was fired as head coach.

On May 5, FIFA rectified its decision and lifted the sanction in its entirety, allowing Messi to participate in the final stretch of the South American qualifiers.

On June 1, Jorge Sampaoli was appointed new coach of the Argentine national team. At the press conference, he stated that Messi was "the best player in the world with many creative variations" and that he planned to put him together with "compatible players".He started by leading two friendlies that same month. On the 9th, Messi did not have a good game at the Melbourne Cricket Ground against Brazil, which Argentina won 1-0, and was absent against Singapore on the 13th, when Argentina thrashed Argentina 6-0 at Singapore's National Stadium.

In the last match, on October 10, with a *hat-trick* by Messi, Argentina beat Ecuador 1-3 in Quito and qualified for the World Cup.

World Cup 2018

On December 1, 2017, the draw for the groups and dates for the 2018 World Cup in Russia took place. The Argentine national team was seeded in group D, together with Iceland, Croatia and Nigeria.

On May 29, 2018, in a friendly against Haiti at the Bombonera in Buenos Aires, Messi scored three of the goals as Argentina won 4-0.

On June 16, after a 1-1 draw against Iceland, in which he missed a penalty, and a 0-3 defeat against Croatia, he scored a goal in the last match against Nigeria, which Argentina won 2-1 and in which he was voted Man of the Match. The team reached second place in the group standings and advanced to the round of 16, where it was eliminated by France, first in Group C, on June 30. Despite his poor performance in the first two and last matches, Messi was nominated for the Puskas Award for his goal against Nigeria, but lost to Mohamed Salah.

On July 14, the AFA announced on Twitter that Sampaoli had stepped down as coach. On an interim basis, and to coach six friendlies, Lionel Scaloni took over the position, who in November was ratified until the next Copa América.

Messi decided not to play any of those matches in which, by Scaloni's decision, no player wore the number 10 jersey. He returned on March 22, 2019, in another friendly against Venezuela at the Wanda Metropolitano stadium in Madrid, which Argentina lost 3-1. Both the team and the player received criticism from various media and former captain Daniel Passarella reproached him for not showing the same "attitude" with the national team as with his club.

America's Cup 2019

In the Copa América on June 15, after losing the first group stage match against Colombia 2-0, Argentina drew

1-1 with Paraguay four days later, thanks to a penalty kick taken by Messi early in the second half. With this result, they had to beat Qatar to advance to the quarterfinals. On June 23, although he did not perform very well, Messi contributed to Argentina's 2-0 win over Qatar, with goals by Lautaro Martínez and Agüero. After Argentina's 2-0 win over Venezuela on June 28, some media criticized Messi's performance, who acknowledged that it had not been his best Copa América, while complaining about the quality of the pitches. In that match, on the other hand, he sang the anthem for the first time, something for which he was repeatedly criticized in his country. After Argentina's 2-0 loss to Brazil in the semifinals on July 2, Messi questioned the refereeing and claimed that the competition was "set up" for the host country to win.

In the third-place match against Chile on July 6, Messi took the free kick that allowed Agüero to score the first goal in a 2-1 victory. However, he was sent off along with Gary Medel in the 37th minute after becoming involved in an altercation with the Chilean defender. After the match, Messi refused to collect his bronze medal and implied in a subsequent interview that his comments after the semi-final had led to his sending off. He later apologized for his comments, but was fined $1,500 and suspended for one game by CONMEBOL, which prevented him from playing in Argentina's next World Cup qualifier.

On August 2, Messi was banned from international soccer for three months and fined US$50,000 by CONMEBOL for his comments against the referee's decisions in the match against Brazil. Due to this ban, he was unable to play in Argentina's friendly matches against Chile, Mexico and Germany in September and October.

America's Cup 2021

On June 14, 2021, Messi scored from a free kick in a 1-1 draw against Chile in Argentina's first group match at the Copa América in Brazil. With this goal, he surpassed Cristiano Ronaldo's mark of 56 free-kick goals and became the active soccer player with the most free-kick goals. He also surpassed Batistuta's record of 38 goals in official matches with Argentina. In the second group stage match against Uruguay on June 18, he assisted Guido Rodríguez's header to secure Argentina's 1-0 victory.

On June 21, he played in the match against Paraguay, which Argentina won 1-0. On June 28, in the last group stage match against Bolivia, he gave an assist to Di María for Papu Gómez's first goal and then scored two more, one from a penalty and one from a set piece, something he had not done since 2018. It was his 148th appearance for the national team, so he surpassed Mascherano's record (147). On July 3, he provided two assists and scored from a free kick in the 3-0 win over Ecuador in the quarterfinals. On July 6, in the semifinal draw against Colombia, he provided his fifth assist of the tournament, a cutback for Lautaro Martinez, equaling his record of five years earlier of nine goal contributions in a single tournament. He later converted a penalty in Argentina's 3-2 shootout win.

On July 10, Argentina defeated Brazil 1-0 in the final at the Maracana. In his fifth international final, Messi won his first title, Argentina's first since the 1993 Copa América and the 15th Copa América in its history. He had been directly involved in nine of the 12 goals scored by Argentina, with four goals and five assists. He was named best player and top scorer of the tournament, an award he shared with Colombia's Luis Díaz. In addition, he equaled two other records: with thirty-four matches played, he equaled the 1953 record of Chilean goalkeeper Sergio Livingstone as the player present in the most matches in the history of the Copa América and, with six participations in that tournament, he became the second Argentinean to reach that number together with goalkeeper Américo Tesoriere, who had achieved it in 1925.

On August 5, the IFFHS included him in Argentina's all-time ideal team.

2022 World Cup Qualifiers

On November 17, 2020, under the direction of Scaloni, and after playing the first four qualifying matches for the World Cup in Qatar, the Argentine national team was in second place in the standings with 10 points, behind Brazil with 12. Against Peru, Messi became the player with the most victories (85) in the history of his national team.

On September 9, 2021, after the suspension of the match against Brazil a few days earlier, the Argentine national team defeated Bolivia 3-0 with a hat-trick by Messi at the Monumental stadium, already in the presence of the public after the COVID-19 pandemic in Argentina. In his 153rd match, Messi reached 79 goals (43 set pieces, 22 penalties, 8 free kicks, 5 with his right foot and 2 headers) with the senior national team, surpassing Pele as top scorer in South American national teams and Luis Suarez as top scorer in Conmebol qualifiers.

After four more matches, against Paraguay with a draw, and victories against Peru and Uruguay in both the first and the second leg, on November 17 at the San Juan del Bicentenario Stadium against Brazil, with a 0-0 final score and with five matches left to play, the Argentine national team mathematically qualified for the World Cup in Qatar. It remained undefeated in the qualifying rounds, after more than two years and twenty-seven matches without being defeated in official and friendly matches.

Finalissima 2022

On June 1, 2022, in the Conmebol-UEFA Champions Cup (nicknamed Finalissima), Argentina beat Italy 3-0 at Wembley Stadium. Messi, who played a very good game, assisted on the first and third goals, as well as shooting three times on goal. At the end of the match, he was named MPV.

Player profile

Style of play

A prolific goal scorer, Messi is known for his finishing, positioning, quick reactions and ability to make offensive runs to beat opposing defensive lines. He can also function in an organizing role, due to his vision and range of passing. He is often referred to as a "magician" for creating scoring situations out of nothing. He is also an accurate free-kick taker, which he began to improve in national team training under Basile, and penalty kick taker, and one of the players with the most goals in history from direct free kicks. He has also been known to score goals by lobbing the ball over the goalkeeper.

Due to his ball skills and short stature (1.69 m), Messi has great agility to change direction quickly and effectively evade opponents' sweeps, which led the Spanish media to start calling him "La Pulga Atómica" (The Atomic Flea).Although not physically imposing, he has significant upper body strength, which, combined with his low center of gravity and balance, helps him withstand physical challenges from opponents; consequently, he has been noted for "faking" little in a sport rife with players who do so. His short but strong legs allow him to execute quick bursts of acceleration, while his quick feet enable him to keep the ball under control at high speeds. His former Barcelona coach, Pep Guardiola, once said that "Messi is the only player who is faster with the ball than without it."

Although he improved his ability with his less skilled leg in his mid-20s, Messi is a predominantly left-footed player: with the outside of his left foot he starts runs by dribbling, while with the inside he finishes plays by finishing or providing an assist or pass.

His pace and technical ability make him known for making long runs with the ball towards the goal, particularly during counterattacks, where he usually starts from the middle or right side of the field. Considered the best dribbler in the world, and one of the best in history, his former Argentina national team coach Diego Maradona has said of him: "The ball stays glued to his foot. I've seen great players in my career, but I've never seen anyone with Messi's ball control." Beyond his individual qualities, he is also a complete and hard-working team player, known for his creative combinations, particularly with former Barcelona midfielders Xavi and Iniesta.

Tactically, Messi plays in a free attacking role. Being a versatile player, he can attack both in the center of the field and on the right side. His favorite position growing up was as an organizer behind two strikers, known as the enganche in Argentina, but he began his Barcelona career playing as a classic left winger. From his first-team debut, he was moved to the right wing by Frank Rijkaard. From this position, he could easily cut back to the center of the field and take shots on goal with his left foot, instead of just throwing crosses to his teammates.

Under Guardiola and subsequent coaches, he has often played in the role of the false nine, positioned as a center forward, but who could prowl the midfield, sometimes dropping into the midfield and bringing defenders alongside him, to create and exploit the spaces left with filtered passes, offensive runs by the other strikers, his own runs or to combine with Xavi and Iniesta. Under Luis Enrique, Messi initially returned to his usual position as a right-sided striker, which was so characteristic of his career, in the coach's 4-3-3 formation, while in recent seasons he himself developed a role as a free and deeper organizer on the field.

Under Ernesto Valverde, he played in a variety of positions. While he occasionally continued to play in a deeper role, where he could make runs from the back into the box, or from the right flank or as a false nine, he was also used in a more central role, in 4-2-3-1 or 4-4-2 formations as a second striker, where once again he was given the freedom to drop deep, link up with the midfielders, orchestrate attacks and create chances for his fellow striker, Luis Suarez.

As his dribbling tendency slowly diminished with age, he began to dictate his play in deeper areas of the field and developed into one of the best passers and organizers of all time. His off-the-ball work and defensive responsibilities also became less as his career progressed: by covering fewer areas on the field and instead conserving his energy to take advantage of more bursts of speed, he improved his effectiveness, movement and positional play, as well as avoiding muscular injuries, despite playing a large number of games per season. Those injuries, frequent in his youth, diminished as he ran less without the ball and followed a strict diet, training regimen and sleep schedule.

With the Argentine national team, he has also played in various positions up front: under different coaches, he has played on the right flank, as a false nine, an all-round striker, a second striker alongside another teammate or in a freer and more creative role as a playmaker or playmaker behind the strikers.

Many point out that Messi, in his last seasons with Barcelona, "does not run" in certain moments of the match. However, different television analyses have shown that this is a typical characteristic of his: he waits for the right moment and places himself in the exact position to take advantage of each play.

Messi-Maradona

With a prodigious talent, in 2006 Messi established himself among the best players in the world before the age of twenty. Maradona considered him, at just eighteen, the best player in the world alongside Ronaldinho, while the Brazilian himself, shortly after winning the Ballon d'Or, commented: "I'm not even the best at Barça", in reference to his teammate. Four years later, after Messi won his first Ballon d'Or, public opinion about his qualities as a player was no longer just about his status in contemporary soccer but also about the possibility of him being the best player in history. The first advocate of that stance was Guardiola who, in August 2009, declared that the Argentine was the best player he had ever seen. In the following years, this opinion gained wider acceptance among experts, coaches, former players, current players and soccer fans, who placed him even ahead of Maradona and Pelé. However, the fact that Messi did not win the FIFA World Cup with Argentina inclined another sector to consider him the best club player in history.

Throughout his career, Messi has been compared to Maradona, due to their similar playing styles of small left-footed dribblers. Initially, he was simply one of several young Argentine players (including his childhood idol Pablo Aimar) who had been called the "New Maradona" but, as his career progressed, he proved his similarity beyond all others and established himself as the best Argentine player since Maradona. Jorge Valdano, who won the '86 World Cup alongside Maradona, said in October 2013 "Messi is Maradona every day."

César Menotti, Argentina's 1978 World Cup coach, echoed the sentiment when he opined that Messi played "at the level of the best Maradona". Other notable Argentines in the sport, such as Osvaldo Ardiles and Diego Simeone, have expressed their belief that Messi surpassed Maradona as the best player in history.

In Argentine society, Messi is generally held in lower esteem than Maradona, a consequence of the difference in their personalities or soccer and media backgrounds. Messi is reserved and simple, an uncomplicated man outside of soccer, the opposite of Maradona. Furthermore, a relevant fact is that Messi never played in the Argentine league, but achieved stardom abroad at a very young age, unlike Maradona, an idol of Boca Juniors, a club with a huge following in Argentina.

In his first stint with the national team, his alleged "lack of passion for the shirt" was criticized by some sectors of his country's fans and press and led to the false perception that he felt more Catalan than Argentine. A repeated criticism was that he did not sing the national anthem, although in 2015 the player explained why. However, as time went by, his bond with the fans grew stronger, and even more so after the team was crowned champions of the Americas against Brazil in 2021.

Despite having lived in Spain since he was thirteen years old, Messi told *La Nación,* "I will always be wherever the national team needs me, wherever I am and whatever the competition. Beyond the bad moments, I am grateful for everything that the national team has allowed me to experience. Now I feel recognized by the general public and I think they value the way I play. I try to keep growing and I dream of giving titles to the national team. What I want most is for Argentina to win.

Messi-Cristiano Ronaldo

Numerous media and soccer fans consider that there is a latent rivalry between Messi and Portugal's Cristiano Ronaldo, mainly because they are contemporaries and have similar sporting records and successes. Between them they have been proclaimed the best players in the world on more than twenty occasions, winning the Ballon d'Or, the FIFA awards, the World Soccer Award and the Globe Soccer Award, among others, in addition to being recognized as the best players of their generation. Some journalists prefer to analyze the playing style of each one, while others study aspects such as economic, advertising, personal and others.

Their sporting competition was linked to that of their respective clubs (Barcelona and Real Madrid) between 2009 and 2018. Ronaldo arrived at the Madrid club on July 6, 2009 and signed for Juventus in 2018. During that time they faced each other at least twice every season in El Clasico, one of the strongest soccer rivalries, and the matches were among the most followed worldwide with millions of spectators, not only because of the importance of the match but also because of the confrontation of their top stars.

In popular culture

Messi is considered one of the best and most influential soccer players, with fans all over the world.

According to a study published by the University of Navarra, which analyzed mentions of Messi in the written press in more than 100 countries, between September 2010 and the end of January 2011, the player was featured in news stories in media around the world at a rate twenty times higher than the average for all footballers playing in the Champions League. A report analyzed for the first time the media impact of the Ballon d'Or award ceremony, which revealed the degree of attention it received in Europe. The flow of information generated by the awarding of the prize to Messi was equivalent to that of the awarding of the Nobel Peace Prize to Liu Xiaobo and double that of the media attention generated by the Nobel Prize for Medicine to Robert Edwards.

In 2011, *Time* magazine included him in its list of people of the year for having "taken the world's most popular sport to even greater heights in its commercial appeal and success, as evidenced by the growing number of American children wearing his Barça jersey in schools". In 2014, *Messi*, a documentary directed by Álex de la Iglesia, was released.

In 2017, he was voted the fifth most influential footballer by British magazine *FourFourTwo*, behind Richard Scudamore, Gianni Infantino, Jorge Mendes and Aleksander Ceferin.

In 2018, according to an analysis conducted by the US consulting firm Hill + Knowlton on his Facebook, Instagram and Twitter profiles, he was the most influential Argentine on social networks and doubled Pope Francis. The list was based on three basic variables: the number of followers, publications and interactions per publication. That year he was considered the most mediatic soccer player in China, according to a study conducted by the sports consulting firm Mailman, which analyzed the digital performance of European soccer in that country.

In 2021, his departure from Barcelona had huge consequences for the club, which lost some €137 million in brand value and brand concept, according to initial studies by valuation consultancy Brand Finance. The financial blow went beyond the club and extended to all of La Liga's accounts and financial balance, as the main impact was felt in the negotiation of audiovisual rights in the following months. The *marketing* that was done generated millions of euros in revenue, in addition to making it an attractive league for every footballer. Income from box office, shirt sales, sponsorships and, above all, television rights in Spain and abroad were seriously compromised. On the other hand, Messi's arrival at PSG led to the development of the club's image at international level. It was revalued by more than 130% since it became known that the player could sign for the Parisian team and also increased the followers on social networks, the sale of shirts and the club's economy in general.

In the streets of different parts of the world there are statues, murals, paintings, graffiti and drawings of the Argentinean. In addition, poems, songs and letters have been written and dedicated to him.

Statistics

The table details the goals, assists and games played in the different official national and international competitions:

Updated as of the last game played on May 21, 2022.

Sources: Goal.com - Transfermarkt - ESPN - Messi.com

Statistical summary

Goals

Data updated as of **February 19, 2022**.

Assistance

Data updated as of **February 19, 2022**.

Goals and assists

Data updated as of the last game played on **February 19, 2022**.

- **Note**
  - A^ Matches played in Copa del Rey, Spanish Super Cup, French Cup and French Super Cup.
  - B^ Matches played in the UEFA Champions League, European Super Cup and Club World Cup.
  - C^ Matches played in the Olympic Games.
  - D^ Matches played in the U-20 World Cup and U-20 South American Championship.
  - E^ Played in the youth teams of Newell's Old Boys (234 goals in 176 games) and Barcelona (105 goals in 107 games) between 1994 and 2005.
  - F^ Friendly matches with Barcelona.
  - G^ Benefit friendly matches.

The 1000 goals

On January 7, 2018, Messi joined the list of players in history with more than 1000 goals, in Barcelona's 3-0 victory over Levante. At Camp Nou, for the eighteenth date of La Liga, he scored his thousandth goal, the first of the match to goalkeeper Oier Olazábal in the 12th minute after a pass or assist from Jordi Alba. The details are: 527 official goals and 34 in friendlies with Barcelona; 61 with the Argentine senior national team; two with the U-23 team and 14 with the U-20 team; plus 23 goals in charity and exhibition games, plus 339 in tournaments he played in the youth divisions of Barcelona and Newell's Old Boys. The statistics could even be higher due to goals that are not included in the count: five goals with Abanderado Grandoli, 18 goals in friendly matches with Newell's youth teams, 24 in preparatory matches with Barcelona's youth teams, one goal in Central Córdoba and 12 in his trial period in River Plate would give a total of 60 more goals.

The 1100 goals

Messi scored his 1100th goal on December 7, 2019, in Barcelona's 5-2 victory at Camp Nou against Mallorca. In total there are: 617 official goals and 35 in friendlies with Barcelona, 70 with the Argentine senior national team, two with the U23 and 14 with the U20, plus 23 goals in charity and exhibition games, plus 339 he scored in tournaments he played in the youth divisions of Barcelona and Newell's Old Boys.

Records

- Top scorer in the history of soccer (21st century): 1174 goals (official, friendly and youth).
- South America's all-time leading scorer in official matches: 758 goals.

- Top scorer in the history of soccer with a single club: 672 goals with Barcelona.
- Top scorer in the history of First Division soccer in a single league: 474 goals (in La Liga) (surpassed Josef Bican with 447 goals - Slavia Prague (417) and MFK Vitkovice (30) - in the Czech league).
- **Most official goals scored** by a player (club and national team) in the 21st century: 1082 goals (759 goals + 323 assists) in 958 games.
- Top assistscorer in official matches (21st century): 323 assists (in 958 matches); 268 with Barcelona, 8 with PSG and 47 with the Argentine national team.
- **Most official goals** (Guinness World Records) scored in a calendar year (club and national team): 86 goals.
- **Most official goals** scored in a single season (club and national team): 82 goals in 69 games in 2011-12.
- **Most official goals** scored in a single year (club): 79 goals in 60 games in 2012.
- **Most official goals** scored in a single season (club): 73 goals in 60 games in 2011-2012 (50 in the Spanish First Division, 14 in the UEFA Champions League, 3 in the Copa del Rey, 3 in the Spanish Super Cup, 1 in the European Super Cup and 2 in the FIFA Club World Cup).
- **Only player in history** to score 50 or more goals in nine different years: 60 (2010), 59 (2011), 91 (2012), 58 (2014), 52 (2015), 59 (2016), 50 (2017), 51 (2018), 50 (2019).
- **Most** FIFA World Player of the Year **winner**: 6 times (4 FIFA Ballon d'Or, 1 FIFA World Player and 1 The Best FIFA).
- **Maximum** Ballon d'Or **winner**: 7 times
- **Maximum** Golden Shoe award **winner**: 6 times

Private life

Since 2007, Messi has been in a relationship with Antonela Roccuzzo, whom he has known since he was a child. He was introduced to her by Lucas Scaglia, her cousin who also played in Newell's youth team. They maintained a long-distance relationship for three years until, after the World Cup in South Africa, she moved to Barcelona. The player made their courtship public in an interview on the program *Hat Trick Barça* in early 2009 and then photographs were published of the couple at the Sitges carnival. They were married in a civil ceremony at the City Center hotel in Rosario on June 30, 2017.

The couple have three sons, Thiago (November 2, 2012), Mateo (September 11, 2015) and Ciro (March 10, 2018), all born in Barcelona. To celebrate his partner's first pregnancy, Messi placed the ball under his jersey after scoring in Argentina's 4-0 win over Ecuador on June 2, 2012, before confirming the pregnancy in an interview two weeks later. Messi announced the arrival of his first child on his Facebook page, where he wrote: "Today I am the happiest man in the world, my son was born and thank God for this gift!" He also tattooed the boy's name and handprints on his left calf. All three were baptized in Rosario.

Since October 2021, the family has been living in Neuilly-sur-Seine, on the outskirts of Paris.

In 2007, Messi created the Leo Messi Foundation, which aims to help children and adolescents at risk, especially in the areas of education and health. Through the foundation, children's playgrounds have been built, charities and sports centers have been refurbished or rehabilitated, among other things. In addition, Messi often participates in benefit events such as friendly matches or fundraising actions, awareness campaigns, donations, visits or solidarity meetings, both for his own foundation and for the F. C. Barcelona Foundation and Unicef. With the F. C. Barcelona Foundation, he reached an alliance to work together.

He has been a Unicef Goodwill Ambassador since March 11, 2010 and, since 2018, UNWTO Ambassador for Responsible Tourism.

His professional affairs are run largely as a family business: his father, Jorge, has been his agent since he was fourteen, and his older brother, Rodrigo, manages his daily schedule and publicity. His mother and another brother, Matías, manage the Leo Messi Foundation and look after personal and professional matters in Rosario.

In March 2020, the World Health Organization called on him, along with other players, to participate in a COVID-19 awareness campaign.

In September, *Forbes magazine* included him in the list of athletes who earned more than 1 billion dollars (840 million euros) during their careers.

Judicial process

In 2013, Messi was investigated for suspected tax evasion. Offshore companies in tax havens in Uruguay and Belize were used to evade €4.1 million in taxes related to sponsorship earnings between 2007 and 2009. Messi, who claimed ignorance of the alleged scheme, voluntarily paid €5.1 million in August 2013. In May 2016, he was tried alongside his father on three counts of tax evasion. On July 6, both were convicted of tax fraud and sentenced to a 21-month prison term and ordered to pay, respectively, €1.7 million and €1.4 million in fines. While the Public Prosecutor's Office did not consider that there were grounds to charge Messi, the Spanish State Attorney's Office became the sole accusing party, despite his statements that he had no knowledge of any of the transactions being made with his money. In front of the judge, he said, "I only dedicate myself to playing soccer."

On May 24, 2017, the Spanish Supreme Court, upon appeal by the player's legal representation, upheld the sentence of the Barcelona Provincial Court and considered him to be the author of three tax offenses for defrauding 4.1 million euros. On June 23, the Prosecutor's Office filed a brief with the Barcelona Court, in which it did not oppose the substitution of the "suspended" prison sentences for a financial penalty. Finally, on July 7, the Prosecutor's Office accepted the substitute penalty established by the judge and Messi paid the fine.

See all our published books here:
https://campsite.bio/unitedlibrary

CPSIA information can be obtained
at www.ICGtesting.com
Printed in the USA
BVHW050319100123
655977BV00020B/293

9 789493 311176